D1201365

SUPER
FEMALE
SCIENTISTS™

SYLVIA EARLE

OCEANOGRAPHER AND CONSERVATIONIST

Xina M. Uhl and Katherine White

Rosen
YA™
New York

Published in 2020 by The Rosen Publishing Group, Inc.
29 East 21st Street, New York, NY 10010

Library of Congress Cataloging-in-Publication Data

Names: Uhl, Xina M., author. | White, Katherine, 1975– coauthor.
Title: Sylvia Earle : oceanographer and conservationist / Xina M. Uhl and Katherine White.
Description: First Edition. | New York : Rosen Publishing, 2020 | Series: Super female scientists | Audience: Grade level for this book is grades 7–12. | Includes bibliographical references and index.
Identifiers: LCCN 2019007240| ISBN 9781725340510 (library bound) | ISBN 9781725340503 (paperback)
Subjects: LCSH: Earle, Sylvia A., 1935– —Juvenile literature. | Marine biologists—United States—Juvenile literature. | Women marine biologists—United States—Juvenile literature.
Classification: LCC QH91.3.E2 U45 2019 | DDC 578.77—dc23
LC record available at https://lccn.loc.gov/2019007240

Manufactured in China

On the cover: This 2009 photo shows renowned oceanographer Sylvia Earle after a dive in Bonaire, in the southern Caribbean off the coast of Venezuela.

CONTENTS

INTRODUCTION

From the time she was a small child, Sylvia Earle has been a passionate advocate for the ocean and the creatures who live within it. On January 3, 2019, she tweeted to her more than 120,000 Twitter followers: "What I love about the ocean is you never know who you're going to see or what you're going to do, but it's always going to be good. It's always going to be a thrill."

At a young age, Sylvia displayed an aptitude for science when she sat beside her family's pond and filled notebook after notebook with observations of the plants and animals that she saw there. She made note of the animals' eating patterns and behavior, drew pictures of them, and collected specimens of plants and animals. Salamanders, tadpoles, and other small creatures became her pets.

It was, perhaps, inevitable that she would become fascinated with the biggest ponds of all: the world's oceans. As she wrote in her book *Sea Change*:

> *The "urge to submerge" came on early and continues, seasoned and made more alluring by thousands of underwater hours, each one heightening the excitement of the last as one discovery leads to another, each new*

Sylvia Earle poses in the water on Padre Island National Seashore in 2006. The seashore, located in Texas, is the longest stretch of undeveloped barrier island in the world.

scrap of information triggering awareness of dozens of new unknowns.

This fascination with water has driven her to accomplish amazing scientific feats throughout her life. She has spent more than seven thousand hours underwater, exploring and studying marine life, and leading more than one hundred ocean expeditions. More than two hundred professional journals and magazines have published her work on topics including ecology and ocean life. Various colleges and universities, including Duke University and Harvard University, provided her with twelve honorary degrees. She was named the first Hero for the Planet by *Time* magazine in 1998. Her nicknames include "Her Deepness" by the *New Yorker* and "Living Legend" by the Library of Congress. She's been named 2009's TED Prize winner and *National Geographic* explorer in residence.

In 1970, Earle captained the first all-female scientific team to live underwater for fourteen days for the Tektite Project, sponsored by the United States government. Upon her return to the United States, she and her colleagues were given a dual honor: a ticker-tape parade and a reception by the White House.

Earle's career started in the 1960s when women's rights only began to be taken seriously. Sylvia Earle, while pursuing her own dreams, helped to pave the way for other female oceanographers by becoming a marine botanist. She was one of the first divers to use scuba (self-contained underwater breathing apparatus) gear. She became the first woman to serve as the chief scientist of the National Oceanic and Atmospheric Administration (NOAA). As an aquanaut, oceanographer, ecologist, writer, and marine biologist, Earle has, indeed, made waves.

Throughout her career and many achievements, Sylvia Earle has maintained a deep love and concern for sea life. As she tweeted on January 31, 2019: "We must take care of the ocean. We must take care of the natural world from the skies above to the depths below."

CHAPTER ONE

A FASCINATION WITH NATURE

Sylvia Alice Earle was born on August 30, 1935, in Gibbstown, New Jersey. Sylvia's parents, Alice and Lewis Earle, were thrilled with the birth of their second child. Both Alice and Lewis were happy people. They had an appreciation for life and many original ideas to share with their children.

The mid-1930s presented a challenging time in America. The crash of the stock market in 1929 set off the Great Depression, a long period of economic downturn in which many people struggled to make a living. President Franklin Delano Roosevelt worked to ease the suffering of the nation through jobs programs.

An unemployed man stands in front of a vacant store in 1935. The Great Depression lasted from 1929 to 1939 and became the industrialized world's worst economic period in history.

In 1938, when Sylvia was three years old, her family moved a few towns away to Paulsboro, New Jersey. The family's new farmhouse was not too comfortable when they first moved in. In fact, it was quite run down. There was no water or electricity, and there were more than a few holes in the roof. Sylvia's father worked night and day to fix it up. Although the farmhouse was not in perfect shape, it did have lots of land surrounding it. Both of Sylvia's parents had grown up on farms, and they wanted their children to experience the same diversions and surprises of farm life. To Sylvia, each day was a new adventure. She had acres of farmland to explore. She discovered old apple orchards, fields of grapevines, and acres of woods. She even had a pond and a creek to examine.

Studying the World

Sylvia showed enthusiasm for science at a very young age. One of her favorite pastimes was investigating the family's pond. She filled a notebook with descriptions of the pond. What really grabbed Sylvia's attention were all of the little creatures that lived in it. She loved the plants and animals that she found in and around the water.

Sylvia would sit as quiet and still as she could, so she would not disturb the pond's natural activity. This is how she would sit for hours, filling her notebooks with facts on the animals' behavior and eating patterns. When she got tired of taking notes, she would channel her more artistic side by drawing the creatures as they scurried, hopped, and swam. Soon, she began to collect specimens—items used for research and testing in experiments. She gathered various plants that blossomed and budded around the pond. She captured insects, salamanders, and tadpoles and brought them home as pets. Just as she did at the pond, Sylvia wrote about how these little animals lived their lives—noting what they ate, when they slept, and what kind of environment they liked the best. Within a short time, the Earle house became Sylvia's first laboratory. Rooms filled up with her collections and research. She had jars everywhere!

Sylvia's parents did not mind. In fact, Sylvia's mother, Alice, encouraged her creativity and interest in animals. Alice also loved animals and nature, and she was glad that her daughter shared her interests. Often, mother and daughter spent afternoons walking together, looking at brightly colored birds while Sylvia collected her beloved plants. In fact, Sylvia's mother was so in love with animals, she was nicknamed the Bird Lady by many of the Earle family's neighbors. She was often seen nursing sick birds back to health, or walking on their farmland, which was filled with tomato plants and huge beautiful gardens, followed close behind by a family of ducks.

A Visit to the Ocean

New Jersey sits along the eastern coastline of the United States, making beach trips a popular pastime. Each year, the Earle family would travel to Ocean

This 1930s-era postcard is from Ocean City, New Jersey, a popular tourist destination with sand dunes, meadows, and beautiful beaches.

City, New Jersey—a favorite vacation spot for many people, even now.

In her book *Sea Change*, Earle shares her very first experience with the ocean:

> *A monstrous wall of green water races my way, hissing, roaring, towering, inescapable, sweeping me into a cascading aquatic mayhem. I am lifted, tumbled, churned, pushed, and fall, gasping, clawing for air. My toes touch sand; a sweet breeze soothes my lungs. I stand choking, face the next advancing wall, and leap into it, exhilarated!*

This is the moment Sylvia Earle fell in love with the ocean. She was only three years old, and still she carries this memory with her as the very beginning of her deep aquatic love.

Until 1948, Sylvia vacationed in New Jersey. She spent days swimming in the ocean, crabbing along the docks, and collecting seashells. When she was at home, she collected plants and animals as she explored during the mornings and afternoons, only to study her great finds in the evening. She had the makings of a future scientist—an instantaneous love for the ocean and a passion to research anything, even things in her own backyard.

Beside the Sea

One would think that a twelve-year-old who loved the ocean would be excited to move right beside it. But Sylvia was less than thrilled when the Earles decided to relocate to Florida.

In 1948, things were not going so well for Sylvia's dad, Lewis, at the factory where he worked. Lewis's job was not as fulfilling as he would have liked, and, after talking with his brother in Florida, he thought starting an electrical contracting business down there might be a change for the better. On top of this, Sylvia's younger brother, Evan, was pretty sick. Both factors caused Sylvia's parents to take action. They believed warmer weather would be good for Evan's health, and they also thought that starting a business would be a great opportunity. Sylvia, however, was hesitant about such a big change. She loved the land surrounding her family's farm, and she was sad to say good-bye. The land, her adventures, and her plant collecting were ending. Thankfully, Sylvia's mood turned around when she got her first glimpse of the Gulf of Mexico.

The town of Dunedin is only a few minutes outside of Clearwater on the western side of Florida. The Gulf of Mexico was Sylvia's new backyard! She was exhilarated. Not only was the water so clear she could see the bottom, but it also revealed all the little plants and animals scurrying along the ocean floor. The water was so different from the grayer, murkier water of New Jersey's shore. Now, Sylvia could spend every day in the ocean. She would never run out of things to explore.

MAN OF THE SEA

Jacques Cousteau (1910–1997) devoted his entire life to sea exploration. He was serving in the French navy when he realized his love for ocean exploration, and only a few years later he was known around the world for it. One of Cousteau's greatest accomplishments came in 1943, when he and French engineer Emile Gagnan

(continued on p. 17)

This 1926 photo shows a diver participating in the New York Zoological Society's debut oceanographic expedition. Early diving suits like this used heavy helmets made from metal.

(continued from p. 15)

perfected the aqualung—a cylinder of compressed air that attached to a face mask, allowing divers to stay under water for hours.

Though he was accomplished as an explorer, Cousteau was just as enthusiastic about sharing his love of the sea with others. His best-known series of books, *Undersea Discoveries of Jacques Yves Cousteau,* was one of Sylvia's favorite reads as a child. She bought every book that came out in the series and read them all more than a few times. She loved the way Cousteau made the ocean come alive on the page. One of Sylvia's favorite movies, *Silent World*, was also done by Jacques Cousteau. Even now, Sylvia still calls Cousteau one of her biggest role models. When Cousteau passed away in 1997, Sylvia knew the world had lost one of the greatest ocean explorers of all time.

A Passion for Adventure

When Sylvia entered school in New Jersey, her teachers noticed her love for science. After moving to Florida and starting at a new school, Sylvia's teachers once again picked up on her deep interest in the sea. All of them worked to help Sylvia learn as much as she could about the ocean and marine animals. Sylvia could not get enough of underwater exploration. So, like many young people who love a certain subject, she turned to books. She read everything she could about deep-water explorers such as Jacques Cousteau and William Beebe. Each adventure she read about spurred more interest and made Sylvia realize one thing: She needed to become a great swimmer.

CHAPTER TWO

THE MAKING OF AN EXPLORER

With all Sylvia's love of water and the creatures that lived within it, the fact that she would become an expert swimmer was almost a given. She had a gift for swimming, and knew exactly what to do to propel herself forward and glide gracefully. Swimming became one of her life's great pleasures.

Learning to Scuba Dive

At sixteen years old, Sylvia had her first dive. A friend's father owned diving equipment and invited her along for a dip in the Weeki Wachee

Sylvia Earle holds a crab as she scuba dives off the Florida Keys. The keys are a chain of coral and limestone islands off southern Florida that extends about 220 miles (355 km).

River in Florida. Keep in mind that this was 1951. Scuba technology was very different than it is today. Sylvia had to wear a heavy helmet that filled up with air and pushed hard on her bare shoulders. The air in the helmet hurt her ears and the suit made it difficult for her to walk through the water. She also had to be attached to a hose while under water—the hose pumped air to her helmet so that she could breathe. Yet Sylvia, always the optimist and adventurer, pushed her discomfort aside and concentrated on the amazing experience she was about to have.

Breathing Underwater

Throughout the 1990s, scuba-diving equipment made some major advances. These improvements and developments greatly improved the scuba diver's underwater experience. Divers could breathe easier, stay under water for longer periods of time, and go deeper into the depths of the sea. One of the biggest innovations was the mixing of gases, such as oxygen and helium, to make air for the diver to breathe. Scientists had been experimenting with different amounts of

(continued on the next page)

(continued from the previous page)

gases for years. After many attempts, they finally were able to successfully recreate the air that we breathe for divers to breathe below the surface of the water. Full face masks, underwater voice communication, and computer systems also brought diving to a great new level. You can probably imagine then that forty years before in the 1950s when Sylvia began to scuba dive, technology was not nearly as advanced.

When her feet touched bottom, she was exhilarated. She looked around and met the flashing eyes of an alligator! She watched as the huge animal opened and closed its mouth a few times. She saw the gator's sharp teeth. Fascinated and enthralled, she stepped toward the animal just as it swished and flicked its strong tail. This movement created such a rush of current that she was almost knocked over. She proceeded on, moving from the middle of the river to the side of the stream. A school of small, gold-brown fish swam around the edge. She walked toward them with bubbles rising all around her. They turned and headed toward her, then swam all around her. Sylvia was amazed! She felt as if she were a part of the river.

Suddenly though, Sylvia felt a wave of dizziness. It felt strange and uncomfortable. She tugged the hose—a sign for wanting to come up—just as someone dived down and pointed for her to return to the boat as quickly as possible. When she was safely out of the water and inside the boat, her friends told her that exhaust fumes from the air generator were getting into the hose and sending her a deadly mix of carbon dioxide, carbon monoxide, and a few other toxic gases. Sylvia was lucky that she was not hurt. As Sylvia relates in *Sea Change*, she learned a big lesson that day: Never take clean air for granted, both above the water and beneath it.

Sylvia's first dive did not quench her love for exploration for very long. Instead, it turned her thoughts to how soon she could go down again. She had a taste for water exploration and she was consumed with when and how she would get to plunge beneath the water's surface and explore the worlds below once again. When she was seventeen, she figured out how she could get more diving experience: She went to college.

During the summer of 1952, when she was only seventeen years old, Sylvia signed up for a marine biology class at Florida State University.

She had yet to even graduate from high school but her knowledge of science and nature extended far beyond the average high school student.

Harold Humm was the marine biology professor for Sylvia's class. His belief was that a student learns more from hands-on experience than from sitting in the classroom. Most of the class time was geared

This wetland is in Florida's St. Marks National Wildlife Refuge. The 70,000-acre (28,327-hectare) refuge was established in 1931 to provide habitat for migratory birds.

to diving expeditions. In 1952, there were no laws as there are now requiring divers to be officially certified. This meant all of the students could take their plunge into the water without much preparation.

The class's first dive was off the shore of St. Mark's Wildlife Refuge in Florida. Harold gave Sylvia two words of advice when she was about to head down into the water: "Breathe naturally." If Sylvia did not breathe naturally, she would experience something called the bends. The medical term for the bends is decompression sickness. It is a very real hazard for divers though it does not happen that often if a diver is careful and well trained.

Basically, the bends occurs for one reason: The longer a diver stays down and the deeper a diver goes, the more nitrogen dissolves in the tissue of the diver's body. If the diver comes up, or ascends, too rapidly the dissolved nitrogen comes out too quickly and forms bubbles in the body's tissues. The diver could experience severe pain, dizziness, blindness, paralysis, or convulsions. This was just one of the things Sylvia was to learn during her first few dives.

Diving Toward Perfection

Earle's first dive in her college marine biology class took place where the water's depth reached only 15 feet (about 4.6 meters). This allowed the diver to reach the ocean floor quickly, and in case of an emergency, return to the surface just as fast. When Earle touched bottom on a mass of soft, brown seaweed, she became elated and immediately glided over to a bouquet of sponges where she spotted a type of fish called a damselfish. Earle had seen this type of fish before during breath-holding dives, but she could stay down longer this time. Staying longer under water allowed the fish time to become comfortable with her presence and she was able to watch as the fish returned to their normal state.

When Earle returned to the surface, she was bursting with enthusiasm. Each dive created this feeling for her, and with only a few diving experiences under her belt, Earle began to formulate a life plan.

What Would the Future Hold?

During the 1950s, women did not have many choices when it came to their careers. It was not like it is

The perfect housewife in the 1950s did the cooking and housework while dressed nicely. *Leave It to Beaver,* a 1950s sitcom, portrayed an iconic view of this lifestyle.

today, where a young woman can be anything she wants to be. Earle was raised during a time when society was less open-minded. Yet Earle did not want to be an English teacher or a nurse, which is what most women became at that time. Earle loved the ocean too much. She decided to go to college to become a marine biology professor. She wanted to share her passion for the ocean with her students.

This was a big decision for a seventeen-year-old girl during the 1950s. But Earle knew what she wanted, and she was determined to achieve her goals. Little did she know exactly how much she would impact those she taught and the world in general.

WORK IN THE WAVES

When Sylvia Earle graduated from high school, she decided to spend a year at St. Petersburg Junior College—she was close to home and her transition into college life was made smoother by this decision. The following year she was ready for a bigger change, so Earle transferred to Florida State University in Tallahassee. The school offered her close to a full scholarship.

Going to College

Harold Humm, Earle's first college professor, also played a big part in her transfer. Earle had kept

Florida State University, located in Tallahassee, Florida, was founded in 1851. Today, the university is known for its commitment to science, technology, humanities, and research.

in contact with Humm and he inspired her to move on to Florida State University. Still a professor there, Humm took Earle under his wing. He saw so much potential and passion in her. He supported her interest in the ocean by teaching her as much as he could. The two forged a great friendship because they both shared a deep love for learning as well as a true love for the sea. Earle also spent a lot of time at the science laboratory because she worked there for extra money.

Earle studied exceptionally hard during her four years at Florida State. She was enthusiastic about learning, and she dedicated herself to absorbing as much knowledge as she could. In 1955, she received her bachelor's degree in marine botany. Few people who knew her were surprised that she wanted to go to the next level and continue learning about the ocean.

Earle was accepted into the master's degree programs at Yale University, Cornell University, and Duke University. Earle chose Duke University in North Carolina for two reasons. First, they offered her a full scholarship, meaning they paid for her tuition, books, and room and board. However, she also picked Duke for a more personal reason. Going there would allow her to work with Harold Humm once again. Professor Humm had moved from Florida State, and Earle wanted another chance to learn from him because she loved the way he taught.

In 1956, Earle earned her master's degree. This huge accomplishment illustrates the immense dedication that Earle had toward her career. She studied algae to earn her master's degree, doing experiments on how it thrives in the ocean. During her college years, Earle was evolving and changing, as were her goals for the future. She realized that she simply did not want to become a professor anymore. She wanted to work directly with the ocean, a career comprised of studying the sea. She wanted to become a marine biologist and explore the ocean as Jacques

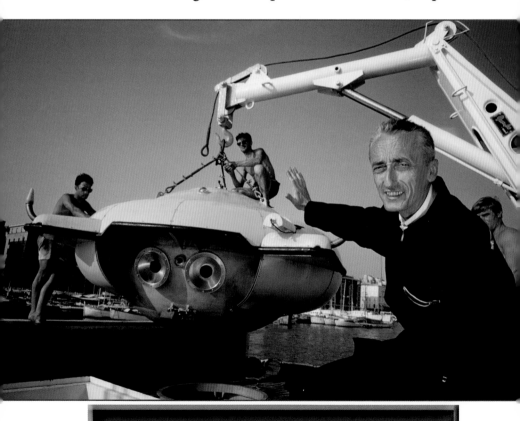

French oceanographer Jacques Cousteau motions at underwater research vessel *Calypso*. His US television series *The Undersea World of Jacques Cousteau* ran from 1968 to 1976.

Cousteau did. Earle knew the hardships that awaited her as a woman trying to become a scientist. But she was up for a challenge.

Encountering Sexism

At Duke, the students in Earle's science classes were mostly men. She was passed up for teaching assistant positions because of her gender. During the course of her education and for years to come, Earle struggled against the popular idea that women should be housewives, not scientists. No one had ever told her that she could not become a marine botanist, but she was given less opportunity than her male counterparts. So, how did Earle handle this? She worked harder. She did not let other people's ideas get her down. Instead, she concentrated on her own dreams and on achieving them. In *Sea Change*, Earle shares her feelings about women scientists and the challenge of society's views: "No matter how competent a woman is, sometimes society rules that only a man will do. I could play by those rules—or not play." Most of the time, Earle chose *not* to play by the rules because she wanted more than anything to be a marine botanist.

Women Who Went Before

Sylvia Earle wasn't the only woman scientist that struggled with the idea that only men should look to science for a career. Two earlier women scientists were both named Mary. Physician and botanist Mary Katharine Layne Brandegee (1844–1920) earned her medical degree from the University of California in 1874. She was one of the first women to be recognized as a scientist. Two species of plants, the *Astragalus laynea* and the *Mimulus layneae*, are named for her. and Mary E. Pennington (1872–1954) was refused a degree in chemistry from the University of Pennsylvania when she earned enough credits for her bachelor's degree. Instead, she received a proficiency degree. After two more years of study, she earned her doctorate in chemistry and she went on to become the chief of the Department of Agriculture's food research lab.

Family Life

At the age of twenty-one, Earle got married. She had met John Taylor, a zoologist, a few years before. After Earle was married, she had no intention of giving up her dreams, so she and John moved back to

34

Sylvia Earle gives a speech alongside her daughter, Liz Taylor. Taylor works with robotics at the Deep Ocean Exploration and Research company, building submersible ocean vehicles.

Dunedin, Florida, into a house right next to Earle's parents. She turned her garage into her laboratory and continued to work on her research from the Gulf of Mexico.

In 1960, Earle turned her attention to motherhood. She gave birth to her first child, a daughter she named

Elizabeth. Just two years later in 1962, Earle's second child was born. Baby John, her little boy, helped to complete the family. Earle loved being a mother, but she also knew she wanted to accomplish more as a scientist. Many times she had two little people beside her, helping to collect specimens and organize the plants in her laboratory as she took scientific notes. In her book *Sea Change*, Earle admits it was very tough at times. She was juggling many roles at once: She was a wife, mother, researcher, and student.

A Botany Career

A marine botanist's job is to study the plant and animal life in a specific underwater area. The job involves looking for certain aquatic plants (plants that live in and around the ocean) and studying their importance to the environment, fish, and other ocean animals. This means the marine botanist studies the ecology of the ocean. Ecology is the study of the relationship between plants and animals and their environment. After Earle earned her master's degree, she began a long-term study on the Gulf of Mexico. She gathered specimens from the water, and then she took them back to her home laboratory, where she would take notes on them. These notes were observations—data collected to learn about a specific topic, in this case marine plants.

Earle went back to school again to get her doctorate so that she could become a marine botanist. So, Earle was once again attending Duke University to earn that degree. Between her schoolwork and her family, Earle had a lot of responsibilities. She was often tired, but she never forgot that her career was incredibly important. In 1964, Earle was offered an amazing opportunity, an opportunity that proved her career was blossoming.

Sailing, Sailing, Over the Bounding Main

In August 1964, Earle was given a huge surprise. The *Anton Bruun*, an old navy ship converted to an exploration vessel for biologists, was about to embark on a journey around the world for six weeks. Earle learned of the voyage from a friend who was planning to go. But, at the last second, her scientist friend could not take the trip. Harold Humm, also a passenger, suggested that Earle take his place. Even though the voyage was an

The *Anton Bruun* conducts fishery surveys near Phuket, Thailand. The vessel was run by the US National Research Foundation.

astounding opportunity to explore water outside of the Gulf of Mexico, Earle was more than hesitant—she had two small children to care for at home. She was also still working on her doctorate, and she didn't know if she could take on another time-consuming task.

However, after talking with her husband, her parents, and her school, she found out everyone was 100 percent supportive of her going—this was, after all, the opportunity of a lifetime!

A Lone Woman

The travel agenda for the trip included many exotic places in and around the Indian Ocean, such as Mombasa, the Amirante Islands, St. Joseph's Reef, the Aldabra group of islands of the Seychelles, Somalia, Dar es Salaam in Tanzania, and Aden in Yemen. Many of these places had yet to be explored by any scientists. On top of this, Earle had yet to travel anywhere outside of the United States. Perhaps you can imagine her excitement when she realized she was about to take the trip of a lifetime. Yet a big challenge lay in her path.

Earle would be sailing around the world for six weeks with an all-male crew. This brought up a variety of different reactions from the crew members. Some scientists who were going on the trip still believed an old sea tale that a woman on board a ship would bring bad luck. It may sound ridiculous that well-educated scientists would believe such a myth, but more than a few people expressed this belief. Fortunately, these people could not prevent Earle from going on the trip.

Her bags were packed, and Earle was ready to go. Yet the day she set sail, she realized that a lot of other people had negative feelings toward her being on board with an all-male crew. A newspaper called the *Mombasa Daily Times* ran this headline: "Sylvia Sails Away with 70 Men, But She Expects No Problem." The article ran beside a photo of Earle coming out of the water dripping wet.

The article was a big blow to Earle, and it caused her to question herself. She went to Harold Humm and expressed her worries. She asked if she was getting in over her head. After all, she had only ever researched the Gulf of Mexico, and she worried that she wouldn't do a good job on the trip. But Harold was an avid supporter of Earle. He saw great talent in her work. He reminded her that sometimes people will have different perspectives, but she could not let it affect her work. That conversation shifted Earle's own perspective.

Sailors struggle to land a large tuna on the *Anton Bruun* in the Indian Ocean around 1963. Tuna can weigh up to 1,800 pounds (800 kilograms) each.

Instead of letting negativity get her down, Earle used the negative energy as fuel to help her work harder. Her first glimpse of the Indian Ocean also made her realize that she had made the right choice. During the trip, Earle worked extra hard to show her abilities. She often rose at 5 am and stayed up recording observations until 3 am. She spent all the time she could in the water, exploring all of the wondrous places below the sea. Earle proved her scientific knowledge on that voyage. During the next four years, she went on four more expeditions aboard the *Anton Bruun.*

CHAPTER FOUR

SCIENTIFIC DISCOVERIES ABOUND

One of Earle's trips aboard the *Anton Bruun* took her toward the Juan Fernandez Islands west of Chile in water that had not been explored scientifically for ninety years. Each scientist aboard the expedition did their own research, but they all shared the same goal, to discover new types of aquatic life.

A New Discovery

During one of her dives, Earle came upon rocks with a mass of thick, pink algae. She had never seen such algae before, so she gathered a specimen

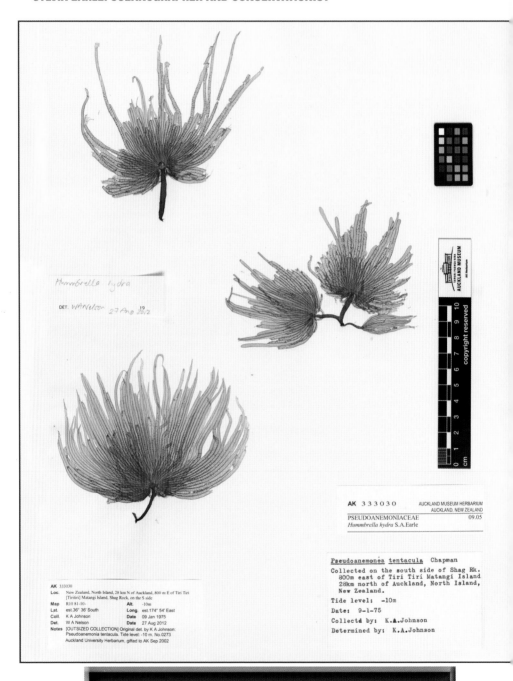

Sylvia Earle's notes appear alongside drawings of her discovery, a red algae she called *Hummbrella hydra* after her mentor, Harold Humm.

before she returned to the surface. Earle found out a few days later that she had found a plant that had yet to be discovered!

It was possible that other explorers had seen the pink algae before but had not bothered to classify it. So technically, Earle had made her first discovery, and it was her job to name the newly found algae. In science, a plant or animal falls into a nomenclature. Nomenclature is a system used in biology for naming kinds and groups of animals and plants. Nomenclature names are always in Latin.

Earle was excited about her discovery, but she was also humble. She realized that in the big picture there were millions of ocean plants that had yet to be discovered. She was, however, very excited about the whole experience.

When choosing a name for the algae, Earle decided that she wanted to pay tribute to a person who had given her an incredible amount of support and knowledge over the years. After much thinking, Earle named the new plant *Hummbrella hydra*. This was her way of saying thank you to her very first college professor and close friend, Harold Humm.

The Ichthyologist

During one of her many trips aboard the *Anton Bruun*, Earle met another female scientist, a rare find back in the 1960s. The two women became fast friends because they shared a lot of the same ideas about science. They also both understood the life of a female scientist because they were both living and experiencing the same difficulties.

"Shark Lady" Eugenie Clark examines deep-water sharks from Suruga Bay, Japan, in 2015. A number of unusual sharks live in deep waters all over the world.

Eugenie Clark is known popularly as the Shark Lady. Within the science world, however, Clark is an ichthyologist—a person who studies ichthyology. Ichthyology is a branch of zoology that studies fish. Clark's favorite fish to study is the shark, and by the time Earle met her, Clark was known as an expert throughout the world on shark behavior. She too had spent thousands of hours under water studying her passion. She dove with sharks all the time, and she had even established her own laboratory.

On a more personal level, Clark had four children, so she and Earle would often find comfort and understanding in one another because of the similarities between their careers and families. They often spoke about the challenges of being a scientist, mother, and wife. Clark showed Earle there was someone else out there who was just as passionate as she was about science, and who also had children at home. In a lot of ways, Eugenie Clark became Earle's role model. A role model is a person someone looks up to for their values, accomplishments, and the way he or she lives life.

The two often went diving together and collected samples. In 1965, Clark invited Earle to work at her laboratory in Sarasota, Florida. Earle accepted the offer and happily became the resident director of the lab. While diving on the East Coast, she met with a variety of sharks: lemon, tiger, hammerhead, bull, and, every once in a while, a huge great white shark showed up. Though the experiments and studies were not directly related to Earle's plant research, she did learn quite a lot about ecology. She was observing and interacting with one of the ocean's fiercest predators, and she saw how the ocean fit together— how each animal and plant learned to live together as part of a balanced system. She learned about the food chain, and it gave her a broader understanding of oceanic life. Earle worked at the laboratory until 1967 while she earned her doctorate at Duke. She completed her doctoral work at the end of 1966.

Endings and Beginnings

In 1965, Earle went through a big change in her personal life. After nine years of marriage to John Taylor, Sylvia and John divorced. The divorce went as smoothly as divorces can. Sylvia and John remained close friends. Earle decided to move herself and the children to Boston for a while and commute to Clark's laboratory.

A crane lowers the submersible vessel *Deep Diver* into the Caribbean Sea near the Bahamas in this 1968 photo.

Soon after, Earle found herself in love again. This time, her love interest was Giles Mead, an ichthyologist. The two got married, and Earle gave birth to her daughter, Gale, in 1968. Including Gale, Giles and Earle had six children between the both of them. The new household was always packed with enormous amounts of activity. But Earle still continued working and diving. In fact, she even dove while she was pregnant with Gale.

On the Sea Diver

In 1968, Earle was invited to participate in a sea exploration in the Bahamas. This time Earle would be under water the entire time. How would that happen? She would be on a submarine, the *Sea Diver*, so all of her dives would start out while she was already under the sea. The one catch was that Earle was pregnant. Before she said yes to the trip, she sought out many doctors' opinions. Each doctor assured her that the baby would be fine even though Earle was five months into her pregnancy.

Another unique thing about this trip was that Earle would be doing all of her "diving" from a dive chamber called *Deep Diver*. The vessel carried two people (actually three with the unborn baby on board). Denny Breese, an expert submariner, and Earle were to dive together inside this vessel. The chamber would submerge into the water, then drop Earle 125 feet (about 38 m) deep. The tiny chamber was a unique technology because when it was dropped into the ocean by a crane, the chamber would match the water pressure outside. So, when

Breese flung open the hatch door, water did not rush in. It merely sat waiting for Earle to slip into the water.

When she emerged from the chamber, Earle again felt the rush that she always felt while diving. She walked along the ocean floor, swimming around checking out the scenery. Overall, the dive was a great success! According to Earle's daughter, Gale, the dive also inspired a deep love in her for the ocean, too, because she was diving even before she was born!

This experience was like a dream come true for Earle. She was able to go deeper into the sea than she ever had before. Little did she know that pretty soon she would be offered an even more amazing chance at sea exploration.

Project Tektite

In 1969, Earle's husband returned home one night to tell her about a flyer he had seen while he was at the Smithsonian Institution that day. The flyer promoted a new project that was about to get underway. The project was phase II of Project Tektite, a study that invited fifty scientists and engineers to live in an underwater hotel of sorts. Sponsored by the US Navy, the Department of the Interior, and the National

Aeronautics and Space Administration (NASA), the project was an incredible opportunity.

The place the scientists would call home for two weeks was rather nice. In fact, a lot of scientists referred to it as the Tektite Hilton, because the interior of the habitat was fully stocked with anything a person would need. A controlled temperature, soft music always playing, a refrigerator, a freezer, a freshwater shower, and comfortable beds were just some of the amenities that the habitat offered. On top of this, the habitat had many portholes, giving it one of the greatest views a scientist could ask for—the ocean lay right outside!

The Difficulties of Gender

Earle was immediately interested in the project because she had been researching how roaming fish (basically, fish in their natural habitat) affect aquatic plants. This project would give Earle the perfect opportunity to observe fish during their daily routine. However, she was once again going to experience a challenge because of her gender.

Earle describes in *Sea Change* the conversation that she had with Dr. James Miller, the director of the project, who said that they hadn't expected women to apply. Earle immediately stressed her deep interest and also shared that she was not alone, that other women scientists wanted a chance. The director had actually received other women's applications and their ideas were so good that the government knew they could not be ignored. Dr. Miller asked Earle what she thought

America's first female aquanauts include, from left: Margaret Ann Lucas, Sylvia Earle, Renate Schlenz True, Alina Szmant, and Ann Hartline before they submerge in the Tektite II program.

about heading an all-female team. Nothing was official yet, but it soon would be.

Controversy flared when the press found out there was a chance that women and men would be living under water together for two weeks. Only a few days after national newspapers ran the stories, Earle was informed that she would head an all-female team! No men would be under water with the women, it was their own project—a major leap forward for women scientists. The team was called Mission 6. They were going to live under water studying plant life for two whole weeks.

Preparing for Tektite

Frustrations left behind, Earle approached Tektite with huge waves of enthusiasm. She was ready for the experience, and when the day finally arrived, she was breathless with anticipation.

The all-female team was made up of:

- Dr. Sylvia Earle, director of Mission 6
- Dr. Margaret Lucas, an ocean engineer
- Dr. Renate True, an oceanographer
- Dr. Alina Szmant, an oceanographer
- Dr. Ann Hurley, an oceanographer

Earle the Housewife?

The Mission 6 all-female aquanaut team provided Earle with great pride—and some frustration, especially when a newspaper article in the *Boston Globe* was run with the headline, "Beacon Hill Housewife to Lead Team of Female Aquanauts." Exactly what frustrated Earle about the article? First, Earle was not a housewife—she was a mother and a wife. Second, by this time, Earle was a distinguished scientist, so she was frustrated with the lack of recognition the article paid to her accomplishments. She also kept thinking to herself that when the all-male team headed down to the bottom of the sea, no newspaper would run an article with the headline, "Beacon Hill Husband to Lead Team of Male Aquanauts." Instead, the article would call him a scientist.

Each woman was intensely devoted to her research and the shared goals that they had set for this project. Earle was specifically excited because the government supplied the mission with the best underwater equipment available. Earle would use a rebreathing system, a new form of underwater technology. The "rebreathing" comes from the fact that the diver carried a small pack on his or her back that recycled breathed air. The system allowed Earle to move through the water without making air bubbles—a usual occurrence with scuba gear. Air bubbles often create a disturbance in the natural environment and lead to the fish having different behavior than normal. Without the bubbles, Earle could gather fantastic notes on the normal behavior of fish with aquatic plants. She also gathered 124 plant species during the two weeks under water!

Overall, each aquanaut accomplished her goal, and the project was considered an astounding success. Their arrival home mirrored what they felt they had accomplished. They rode in a tickertape parade, and they were invited to lunch at the White House.

CHAPTER FIVE

A RECOGNIZED SCIENTIST

A long with scientific recognition, the Tektite project also caused Earle to become a public figure. Suddenly, she found herself in the forefront of the public eye. She was being promoted as an ocean advocate—a person who talks to the public about the importance of a specific subject, trying to raise awareness, motivation, and support. At first, Earle had mixed feelings about her new popularity with the public.

In the Public Eye

Earle had always kept herself out of the public eye. She was a scientist. Her passion was the ocean and her laboratory. She enjoyed expeditions and exploring far-off places, always thankful she was gaining scientific experience. She never thought about becoming a scientific celebrity, and for a long time, she had mixed feelings about public appearances. After Tektite, though, Earle had little choice but to accept the hundreds of public speaking and interview invitations she received. After a few interviews, Earle had quite a shift in her attitude toward the media.

Earle started to view each interview the same way she viewed her voyages: as an exploration. In 1970, Earle appeared on a variety of television shows. She was interviewed by some of the best news personalities of the times, such as Barbara Walters and Hugh Downs. In each interview, she worked hard to shift the lighter questions, like "Did you see any sharks?" to more scientific ones. Earle worked to send more important messages about the ocean, such as the need for more exploration and the need for environmental cleanliness. Overall, she found the whole experience challenging and invigorating.

In fact, throughout 1971, Earle found herself at speaking engagements and lecture series almost every week. At each event she tried to send a strong

News personality Barbara Walters hugs her *Today Show* cohost Hugh Downs when she left the show in 1976. She remained active in television until 2014.

message to the public. She stressed the importance of oceans and oceanic life. She talked of the need to keep the oceans healthy as well as the need to keep studying and exploring them. Once again, Earle's positive attitude opened doors and paved roads to new opportunity.

In 1971, Earle received a call from William Graves, an editor at *National Geographic*. The magazine wanted her to write a story about her experiences during the Tektite project. Earle questioned whether or not she wanted to write an article. She realized that as a scientist it was hard to straddle both the scientific world and the public one simultaneously. Often, scientists lost respect for the person who chose "popular science."

On a more personal level, Earle also worried about her ability to reach the public. She used such incredibly scientific words when she talked about science that she wondered if she would be able to hold a reader's attention. However, after much thought she decided to write the article, because she thought it was a wonderful opportunity to teach people about the ocean.

Sylvia Earle is shown here in a 1970 photo. The photo's original caption notes that she is "5 ft 3 in [160 cm], 110 pounds [50 kg] and pretty."

Danger Below

Earle worked for a long time on her article for *National Geographic*. She chose to write about a potential disaster that occurred during Tektite. In *Sea Change*, Earle shares her knowledge about diving.

About the Ocean

The world's oceans are not only a source of wonder, they are also vital to Earth's continuing existence. The oceans cover 71 percent of Earth's surface, hold 97 percent of Earth's water, and contain under the surface 8 percent of all life on Earth. The first plants on Earth, the algae, developed in the sea 3.5 million years ago. Coastlines around the world make up about 313,200 miles (504,000 km), enough to circle the equator twelve times, and the average depth of the ocean is 12,450 feet (3,795 m). At the deepest point in the ocean, the pressure is more than eight tons per square inch, or the equivalent of one person trying to support fifty jumbo jets, making it a dangerous place for humans who dare to explore it.

She says that when diving, the biggest danger does not come from sharks, jellyfish, or other creatures in the deep sea. She says that the most fatal mistake a diver can make is to panic.

During one of her Mission 6 dives, Earle experienced a moment that could have lead to her death. She was out swimming and gathering observations when she realized she was out of air. Rather than panic, Earle swam toward her diving partner—always a must while diving—and signaled to her partner that she was out of air. Her partner that day was Margaret Lucas, a woman whom everyone called Peggy. When Earle gave the sign to Lucas, the other diver reacted calmly. She and Earle simply made their way back to the habitat while buddy breathing. Buddy breathing is a standard procedure in diving. It consists of passing a mouthpiece containing air back and forth between divers. Though simple, buddy breathing is very important during a crisis.

That day Earle and Lucas arrived back to the habitat perfectly safe, sharing the mouthpiece. A potentially fatal dive was turned around because both divers reacted calmly and without panic.

Unwilling Aquababes

When Earle saw her article published in *National Geographic* in 1971, she was pretty unimpressed with the title. The article was entitled "All Girl Team Tests the Habitat." Earle was thirty-four years old. The youngest person on the voyage to the deep sea was twenty-three years old, and all of them were scientists. Earle was once again frustrated with the media's lack of respect for women scientists. She realized that *National Geographic* was following the same wave of interest that used the nickname "Aquababes" to describe female scientists. After some thought, Earle chose to be positive, so she viewed the article as a chance to reach two million readers and share her love for aquatic life.

The SCORE Project

By 1975, most underwater labs, like the habitat, had been dismantled. However, one underwater laboratory called *Hydrolab* was still being used. In April 1975, Earle was chosen as a team leader for an expedition called SCORE Project. SCORE stands for Scientific Cooperative Operational Research

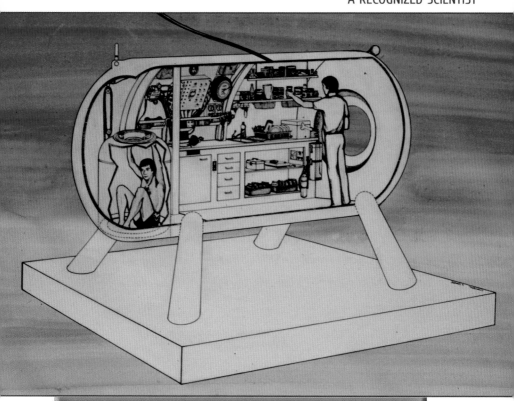

The inner workings of the *Hydrolab* are shown here. The vessel was designed to allow divers to live and work on the ocean floor for seven days.

Expedition, and during this exploration, Earle was going 250 feet (about 76 m) deep into the ocean in a tiny submarine.

Back in 1970, when the original habitat program began, Ed Link, a scientist, dreamt of a day when divers would be able to explore greater depths. He soon partnered with Seward Johnson, an industrialist and sailor. The two men began work on an underwater vehicle. By 1975, they had perfected the *Johnson Sea-Link I* and *Johnson Sea-Link II* underwater vehicles. The inventions were commonly called bubble subs, because even though they were much smaller than submarines, the vehicles had a large bubble sphere. The sphere was made out of acrylic, and it allowed a driver and a diver to clearly observe the deepest depths in the ocean. However, before Earle could plunge in, she had to use a decompression chamber.

Time to Decompress

During Tektite, Earle and her four team members had to sit in a decompression chamber for twenty-one hours before they could step back on land. What's the reason for this?

Water pressure increases with the depth of the water. When a diver is in very deep water, there is more water above, pressing down on him or her. This pressure can cause a variety of reactions ranging from feelings of intense euphoria to convulsions. None of these extreme feelings are good for a diver's health. Decompression chambers reduce the pressure within the diver's body by changing oxygen and nitrogen levels. The chamber mimics the ocean's depth, easing the diver's body into increased pressure. The whole point is to slow down the process of pressurizing the body—slower speed gives the diver's body time to adjust without any unhealthy side effects.

Decompression was usually a lengthy process, and scientists were working on shortening the time a diver had to spend decompressing after a dive. In April 1975, Earle emerged from the decompression chamber of the bubble sub, already fifty feet (about fifteen meters) below the ocean's surface. While inside the submarine, her body had already adjusted to the pressure normally felt at fifty feet below the surface. However, on this day Earle's reaction to the water was a test in itself. Never before had anyone attempted to decompress in the middle of the ocean—divers always decompressed on land. Earle tested a theory that had only been tested before in nonhuman experiments. Her dive proved that a diver experienced less pressure if he or she started out deeper in the water. In other words, decompression chambers could be used for shorter periods of time if the diver plunged into the water at deeper levels. This cut down the time spent in a decompression chamber, making diving far easier.

Thar Be Whales!

In 1977, Earle received another amazing invitation. Katy and Roger Payne, two biologists who focused on whale studies, invited Earle and her children along on a trip to the Hawaiian Islands. The couple had been doing research on whales for many years, and they thought Earle would enjoy the chance to get to know another creature that lived in the ocean. Earle was more than excited about the chance to swim with the huge creatures. The three scientists would be studying the humpback whale.

Some might think that humpback whales are the most interesting fish in the sea. But actually, they're not fish. Humpback whales, like all whales, are warm-blooded animals, meaning they are actually mammals. They have stocky bodies and flat, broad heads. Full-grown males average 42 feet (about 13 m) in length and weigh about twenty-five tons. The female humpback whale is larger. They average about 45 feet (about 14 m) in length and weigh about thirty-five tons. Grooves run along the underside of humpbacks from their chins to their navels. Both sexes have flippers that are long

A young male humpback whale (*left*) swims beside an adult female humpback (*center*) while a diver (*right*) provides scale.

and winglike with bumps on the front edges. They also have blowholes on the top of their heads to help them breathe when they come to the surface for air.

Though Earle had a great amount of respect for whales, she was wracked with nervousness as she first got into the water, mainly because she was not used to swimming with such large creatures. Two photographers, Chuck Nicklin and Al Giddings, were out with her to take pictures of their adventure. All three of them were in the water when all of a sudden a pregnant female whale shot up from the ocean's depth. Despite her bulk, the whale moved really quickly. Al Giddings was busy taking pictures, and he did not notice that the whale was heading straight for him. Humpbacks are known to be very gentle mammals, but their size can pose big problems.

The whale's flipper was heading right for Al's head. The photographer was so taken by the moment that he did not even realize what was happening. Earle felt a pang of fear turn to relief as the whale's flipper flicked upward and missed his head. Earle relaxed and learned to trust the whales, and the rest of the diving went smoothly. She gained enormous amounts of observations and insight into the lives of whales during the three months that she dove with them in and around Hawaii.

When Earle returned from her trip to Hawaii, she decided to move her family to Oakland, California, to follow up the project. She was in the process of her second divorce, and she thought the change would be good for her whole family. Though emotionally drained, Earle took a few months to regain a balanced life. She worked on her humpback whale observations and spent a lot of time with her children. She relaxed with them, enjoying their active and creative energy.

NEW IDEAS, NEW EFFORTS

One of Earle's first projects after moving to California was something entirely new for her. She would be diving 1,250 feet (381 m) into the ocean—deeper than she had ever gone before. Not only that, but the dive would be the deepest untethered human dive in history! As an untethered dive she would not be attached to any lifelines or cranes during the dive.

A Television Star

Al Giddings, the same photographer that Earle worked with in Hawaii, came to her and proposed the original idea. He thought it would be a good way to get people excited about ocean exploration again. At that time, a lot of scientists were frustrated with the lack of popularity surrounding ocean exploration. Al and Earle were ready to do something about it. They got ABC television and *National Geographic* interested in the project. The television station was going to do a two-hour special on the event and *National Geographic* would do a huge article on it. They were motivated and excited, and they had the technology they needed to complete their mission.

Jim Jarrett's Suit

The concept of the JIM suit, named after diver Jim Jarrett, was originally thought of in 1965 in Britain. However, it took another ten years before the suit became practical and popular. By 1979, when Earle began to train to use the suit, the JIM had gone through many variations. Phil Nuytten, who owned the patent for the suit—meaning he was the only person at that time who could produce and sell it—was interesting in studying how the suit performed during Earle's untethered dive.

(continued on p. 75)

The JIM suit was the first modern commercial atmospheric diving suit. It weighed 910 pounds (413 kg) and worked to 1,500 feet (457 m) deep.

(continued from p. 73)

Learning to use the JIM suit was not an easy task—it required special training to master its complex requirements. The suit was heavy and very mechanical in its design. It was not free moving, and it looked and moved much as a robot would. Divers had to learn to walk in the suit and move about in it as well.

Earle would be using a diving suit called a JIM suit to help her reach the deepest depths of the ocean. Earle worked ferociously at mastering the JIM, and with a few months of preparation and a few test dives, she was ready for the big day.

On October 19, 1979, Earle made her adventure 1,250 feet (381 m) into the sea. Earle spent two and a half hours exploring the sea that day. She even planted an American flag on the ocean floor! Although she had enjoyed such a long dive, she was sad that she had to return to the surface. As always, she wanted to stay down there forever to swim about, exploring the sea.

Going Deeper than Ever Before

By 1981, Earle was ready to branch out and work for deep-ocean exploration, but in a different way than she had in the past. She accomplished this by starting her own business, called Deep Ocean Technology. Her business partner was her new husband, Graham Hawkes—they had married in 1980. The primary goal of the company was to build vehicles that helped explorers move through the ocean. The couple ran the business out of their home, and though the company had a bit of a rough start, they hit success in 1984 when they unveiled a major leap in ocean diving technology.

The new ocean vessel, or submersible, was called *Deep Rover*, and it was a one-man sub that could go 3,000 feet (about 914 meters) deep. The sub was a huge leap for divers, because they could drive the vehicle and explore greater depths for longer periods of time.

In 1985, Earle and her husband took *Deep Rover* out for a spin. They each went down separately 3,300 feet (1,006 meters) into the Pacific Ocean, a distance that was unequalled at the time. During Earle's second dive in November 1985, she came face to face with a huge surprise. She was down observing the behavior of dolphins when she spotted a Soviet submarine. At that time in history, the relationship between the United States and the Soviet Union was

Sylvia Earle floats alongside the *Deep Rover* submersible vessel during a 2009 test dive.

not very friendly, so when the sub approached *Deep Rover*, Earle became nervous. Luckily, all the crew did was wave to Earle as they passed by. Earle waved back with an uneasy smile and a great sigh of relief.

Earle and Graham's company had a major upswing after *Deep Rover*. They had entered the ocean-vehicle market and their company was gaining recognition. The couple had been working on a new vehicle called *Deep Flight* for many years, and in 1988, they received major funding from IMAX, a film company. In exchange for the use of the vehicle to film under water, the company supplied Deep Ocean Technology with enough money to complete work on this new project. *Deep Flight* was different from *Deep Rover* because it was even easier to handle. It also carried only one person, but the vehicle was much more simple in design. Like *Deep Rover*, though, *Deep Flight* could only go about 3,000 feet (914 meters) deep.

By the end of the 1980s, Earle had accomplished a lot. She had started a new company and successfully completed two new ocean submersibles. She was also beginning to publish a lot of her work in journals and magazines. The 1980s, like so much of Earle's life, had been full of adventure and passion for her career.

EARNING ACCOLADES

I n the 1970s, when the Tektite project had ended, Earle had been launched into the public eye by public demand, but not by choice. In the 1990s, Earle reentered the mainstream media with one goal in mind: She wanted to educate the public about oceans and help keep them healthy and safe. She appeared on *Good Morning America* in 1994, 1996, 1997, and 2001. She was also featured on other TV shows to rally support for her cause. She wrote books that explained the fragile state of the oceans, including a series of children's books about fish and her own dives with the help of *National Geographic*. Earle wanted to make a difference.

Sylvia Earle (*in blue*) stands next to US president George W. Bush (*center*) as he signs a 2006 proclamation to establish the world's largest protected marine reserve northwest of Hawaii.

In Charge

In 1990, President George H. W. Bush asked Earle to head the National Oceanic Atmospheric Administration (NOAA). Earle, always up for a challenge, accepted the position with high hopes. She moved her family to Washington, DC, and she plunged into her new job.

The goal of NOAA is to study human behavior in relation to the oceans. This meant Earle's job was to figure out how to help humans and fish lead a more peaceful and healthy coexistence. At the time, the fish population was being depleted at an alarming rate, and it was upsetting the balance of nature. Earle found herself flying to Japan and Iceland to speak with these countries' leaders about these pressing matters. The more she learned, the more worried she became. Earle cared deeply for oceans and they were being destroyed at a rapid rate.

Earle served the NOAA until her resignation in February 1992. She had a new goal to follow and wanted to focus all her energy on it.

Pollution and the Ocean

One of Earle's biggest concerns about the sea (and one of the reasons she became an ocean activist) was how polluted the sea had become. Many times on television, Earle shared how the amount of litter had increased during her dives—steadily, through the 1960s. She

(continued on p. 83)

In 2012, Japanese researchers make use of the *Shinkai 6500* submersible vessel in the Pacific Ocean near Guam.

(continued from p. 81)

often spoke of her experiences in some of the most remote places, where she would see plastic netting attached to coral reefs. Many ocean dwellers are affected by the tons of trash being dumped into the ocean each year. Each piece of pollution takes away from the ocean's natural balance and usually creates a loss of marine life.

Plastic pollution in the ocean has worsened over the years, until today the Great Pacific Garbage Patch floats in the ocean between California and Hawaii. Made of garbage generated by humans, it has more than 1.8 trillion pieces of plastic, or 250 pieces of trash for every human being on earth!

Japan's Accomplishment

In 1992, while Earle was beginning her crusade to rid the oceans of pollution, she was offered a chance to go 13,065 feet (about 3,982 m) deep. Diving at that depth was almost unbelievable to Earle—the deepest she had ever been was 3,300 feet (1,006 m). She could not imagine what the ocean would be like so far down. Earle, always ready for a challenge, packed her bags and headed to Japan where she would meet the new, amazing *Shinkai 6500*.

The *Shinkai 6500* was a stunning accomplishment for Japan. The vessel went deeper and faster and glided more smoothly than any other submersible in the world. Earle was astounded at how comfortable her ride down was. The pilot even asked her if she wanted to listen to a compact disc (CD)!

It took Earle an hour and a half to go down 2.5 miles (about 4 km). This was the quickest ride she could imagine. The *Shinkai 6500* cruised around as Earle caught sight of blazing blue jellyfish and other glowing creatures. The whole experience made her realize again just how vast and amazing the ocean was. When she returned to the surface, her activism had deepened. She felt even more passionate and determined to help her oceans. Only a few years later, she saw magnificent results.

A Hero for the Planet

In 1998, *Time* magazine awarded Earle with an amazing achievement. She was named *Time*'s Hero for the Planet. Roger Rosenblatt's article, "Call of the Sea," described Earle in great detail: "She is a small-

Sylvia Earle (*left*) and an unidentified diver make use of fish reference charts as they dive in the Florida Keys National Marine Sanctuary in July 1997.

boned, fearless woman with a kid's keen face, deep brown eyes set far apart, and a jaw of character, like the young Katharine Hepburn's. Sometimes the alertness in her eyes and the quick, broad smile are disconnected."

Earle was excited about the award, and she knew she deserved it. She had given the world great knowledge of the sea. But she was also humble about it, because she never sought fame or recognition for her adventures. Each exploration was just simply another chance to learn about the sea, the place she loved best of all.

In 1999 she was appointed *National Geographic's* explorer in residence. She continued with her work as always. In 2009, she was awarded the TED Prize that recognizes her work as an oceanographer who has led fifty-plus expeditions, and spent in excess of 7,000 hours underwater. In 2010, Earle began leading Mission Blue, a worldwide effort to educate the public about their oceans and establish marine protected areas called Hope Spots. Made of respected scientists, activists, and media professionals, Mission Blue works with more than two hundred ocean conservation groups across the planet.

Sylvia Earle attends the 2018 *National Geographic* Awards in Washington, DC. She has been designated a *National Geographic* explorer in residence.

These days, Earle concentrates most on sharing her experiences with the world. She has lived a true scientist's life. Her adventures and explorations have taken her to some of the most fascinating parts of the world, the world beneath. Her passion for her work is extraordinary and thought provoking. She challenges individuals to look out at the world the same way she does. She challenges everyone to see the unknown adventures everywhere.

Timeline

1935 On August 30, Sylvia Alice Earle is born in Gibbstown, New Jersey, to Lewis and Alice Earle.

1938 Young Sylvia and her family move to Paulsboro, New Jersey, to live on a farm. The farm's pond inspires Sylvia's first scientific investigations.

1951 Sylvia experiences her first breathing-assisted dive in the Weeki Wachee River in Florida.

1952 At seventeen years old, before graduating from high school, Sylvia enrolls in a marine biology class at Florida State University. There she meets Harold Humm, her first professor and a lifelong friend.

1955 Earle earns her bachelor's degree in marine botany from Florida State. She decides to continue her education by pursuing a master's degree at Duke University.

1956 Earle earns her master's degree in marine botany from Duke University.

1964 Earle accepts a trip to travel all over the Indian Ocean aboard the *Anton Bruun*. This is her first scientific exploration into foreign waters.

1965 Earle discovers a new type of algae in a group of islands near Chile. She names the algae *Hummbrella hydra*, after her lifelong friend Harold Humm.

<u>1968</u> Earle participates in an exploration called the Man-in-the-Sea Project. She dives from a small submarine called the *Deep Diver*. At this time, she's pregnant with her daughter Gale.

<u>1970</u> Earle heads an all-female team of scientists on the Tektite Project, in which she and four other women scientists live in the ocean for two weeks.

<u>1979</u> On October 19, Earle tests out the JIM suit and dives 1,250 feet (381 meters) into the ocean. She breaks the record for the deepest untethered dive in history.

<u>1984</u> Earle's company, Deep Ocean Technology, meets with huge success when it unveils *Deep Rover*, a fantastic new underwater submersible.

<u>1990</u> President Bush asks Earle to head the National Oceanic Atmospheric Administration (NOAA).

<u>1992</u> Earle goes 13,065 feet (3,982 meters) deep in a

Glossary

advocate A person who talks to the public about the importance of a specific subject, trying to raise awareness, motivation, and support.

aquanaut A term used for divers who visit the ocean, much as astronauts visit space.

bends An illness that occurs when a diver's blood receives too much nitrogen; also called decompression sickness.

cultivate The act of helping to inspire growth or an interest in something.

decompression chamber A chamber used to reduce the pressure within a diver's body by changing oxygen and nitrogen levels.

ecology The study of the relationship between plants and animals and their environment.

ichthyology A branch of zoology that involves the study of fish.

marine botanist A person who studies plant and animal life in a specific area and looks for what kind of plants live in the ocean and why they are important to the environment, fish, and other ocean animals.

nomenclature A system used in biology to classify different kinds and groups of animals and plants.

role model A person someone looks up to for his or her values, accomplishments, and the way he or she lives life.

specimen An item used for research and testing in experiments.

submersible A vessel used for underwater exploration, much like a very small submarine.

TED A nonprofit group designed to use technology, entertainment, and design to solve global issues.

For More Information

The Coral Reef Alliance
1330 Broadway, Suite 600
Oakland, CA 94612 USA
(888) CORAL-REEF (267-2573)
Email: info@coral.org
Website: http://www.coral.org
Facebook: @coralreefalliance
Twitter and Instagram: @coral_org
The alliance works with local communities in coral
    reef areas worldwide to protect their coral reefs.

Greenpeace Canada
33 Cecil Street
Toronto, ON M5T 1N1
Canada
(800) 320-7183
Website: https://www.greenpeace.org/canada/en
Facebook: @greenpeace.canada
Twitter: @GreenpeaceCA
Instagram: @greenpeace_canada
Greenpeace works to protect the world's oceans
    through vocal protests and activism.

National Oceanic and Atmospheric
   Administration (NOAA)
1401 Constitution Avenue NW, Room 5128
Washington, DC 20230
Website: http://www.noaa.gov
Facebook, Twitter, and Instagram: @NOAA
The agency's mission involves protecting and
   studying nine key areas: weather, climate,
   oceans and coasts, fisheries, satellites, research,
   marine and aviation, charting, and sanctuaries.

The National Women's Hall of Fame
76 Fall Street
PO Box 335
Seneca Falls, NY 13148
(315) 568-8060
Website: https://www.womenofthehall.org
Twitter and Instagram: @WomenoftheHall
The organization honors and celebrates the
   achievements of special American women.
   The website hosts the biographies of numerous
   celebrated women from the past and present.

Oceana
Email: info@oceana.org
Website: http://www.oceana.org
Facebook, Twitter, and Instagram; @oceana

This international organization focuses on
protecting and restoring oceans worldwide.

The Ocean Conservancy
1300 19th Street NW, 8th Floor
Washington, DC 20036
(800) 519-1541
Website: https://oceanconservancy.org
Facebook and Instagram: @oceanconservancy
Twitter: @ourocean
This charitable organization protects the world's
oceans by advocating for conservation laws,
hosting educational programs, and running
beach cleaning events.

Society for Canadian Women in Science and
Technology
#311 – 525 Seymour St.
Vancouver, BC V6B 3H7
Canada
(604) 893-8657
resourcecentre@scwist.ca
Website: http://www.scwist.ca
Twitter: @scwist
This nonprofit organization is dedicated to
promoting and empowering girls and women in
science, engineering, and technology.

Earle, Sylvia A. *Blue Hope: Exploring and Caring for Earth's Magnificent Ocean.* Washington, D.C.: National Geographic, 2014.

Earle, Sylvia A. *Dive: My Adventures in the Deep Frontier.* Washington, D.C.: National Geographic Society, 1999.

Earle, Sylvia A., and Joelle Delbourgo. *Sea Change: A Message of the Oceans.* New York, NY: Fawcett Books, 1995.

Earle, Sylvia A., and Linda K. Glover. *Ocean: An Illustrated Atlas.* Washington, D.C.: National Geographic, 2009.

Faulkner, Nicholas. *Top 101 Women of STEM.* New York, NY: Britannica Educational Publishing, 2017.

Johnson, Rebecca L., and Sylvia A. Earle. *Journey Into the Deep: Discovering New Ocean Creatures.* Minneapolis, MN: Millbrook Press, 2011.

Popova, Maria, and Claudia Zoe Bedrick. *A Velocity of Being: Letters to a Young Reader.* New York, NY: Enchanted Lion Books, 2018.

Rizzo, Johnna. *Ocean Animals: Who's Who in the Deep Blue.* Washington, D.C.: National Geographic, 2016.

Rowell, Rebecca. *Sylvia Earle: Extraordinary Explorer and Marine Biologist.* Minneapolis, MN: Core Library, 2016.

Skeers, Linda, and Livi Gosling. *Women Who Dared: 52 Stories of Fearless Daredevils, Adventurers & Rebels.* Naperville, IL: Sourcebooks, Inc., 2017.

Baker, Beth. *Sylvia Earle: Guardian of the Sea.*
    Minneapolis, MN: Lerner Publishing Group, 2000.

Earle, Sylvia A. *Sea Change: A Message of the
    Oceans.* New York: Fawcett Books, 1995.

Earle, Sylvia A. (@SylviaEarle). "We must take
    care of the ocean. We must take care of the
    natural world from the skies above to the depths
    below." Twitter, January, 31 2019. https://
    twitter.com/SylviaEarle
    /status/1091155893931016193.

Earle, Sylvia A. (@SylviaEarle). "What I love about
    the ocean is you never know who you're going
    to see or what you're going to do, but it's always
    going to be good. It's always going to be a thrill."
    Twitter, January, 3 2019. https://twitter.com
    /SylviaEarle/status/1080909632787247109.

Gradwohl, Judith. Smithsonian Institution. "Ocean
    Planet: Oceanic Facts." Retrieved April 12, 2019.
    http://seawifs.gsfc.nasa.gov/OCEAN_PLANET
    /HTML/education_oceanographic_facts.html.

Mission Blue. "About Us." Retrieved on April 12,
    2019. https://mission-blue.org/about.

National Geographic Explorer. "Where Does

Oceanographer Sylvia Surf the Web?" Retrieved
April 12, 2019. http://www.nationalgeographic
.com/bookmarks/earle.

Ocean Cleanup, The. "The Great Pacific Garbage
Patch." Retrieved April 12, 2019. https://www
.theoceancleanup.com/great-pacific-garbage
-patch.

TED. "Sylvia Earle Oceanographer." Retrieved on
April 12, 2019. https://www.ted.com/speakers
/sylvia_earle.

Index

About the Authors

Xina M. Uhl is the author of numerous books, lessons, and assessment questions in the educational field. A graduate of Arizona State University (BA) and California State University Northridge (MA), she enjoys reading and researching at every opportunity. Learn about her fiction at her blog.

Katherine White is a freelance editor and writer. She lives in Jersey City, New Jersey.

Photo Credits

Design and Layout: Nicole Russo-Duca; Photo Researcher: Nicole DiMella